Sponsored by THE TIMES

Imperial War Museum 15 September–13 November 1994
Lambeth Road
London SE1 6HZ

Flowers East 15 September–30 October 1994
199/205 Richmond Road
London E8 3NJ

Peter Howson: **BOSNIA**

IMPERIAL WAR
MUSEUM

Published by the Imperial War Museum,
Lambeth Road, London SE1 6HZ

© The Trustees of the Imperial War Museum
and the authors 1994

Designed by James Campus

Printed by Grillford Limited, Bletchley,
Milton Keynes, MK1 1ND

A catalogue record for this book is available
from the British Library

ISBN 1 870423 13 5

Cover: *Study for Travnik,* 1993-94 (detail)
Frontispiece: *Fleeting Glimpse,* 1993-94

Introduction

The Times is honoured to be involved in ensuring that there is this
extraordinary artistic record of the tragic events in Bosnia. Sponsoring
the official war artist in Bosnia has both reinforced *The Times'*
commitment to the arts and added invaluably to *The Times'* coverage of
the war. The role of the official war artist is to record not only the horrors
of war but the heroism and dignity too. During the First World War, when
Sir Muirhead Bone toured the battlefields of the Somme, his art was one
of the few means of communicating the reality of war to those at home.
Today, when images of human suffering loom regularly on our television screens and in our newspapers, the painter has not lost the power
to move.
Peter Howson is one of Britain's finest contemporary artists. His often
violent images and his ability to invest ordinary men and women with
heroic dignity, made him an obvious choice to chronicle the catastrophe
in Bosnia. His magnificent response to the challenge marks an important
development in his own work, particularly in his more vibrant palette.
These pictures are shocking works of historical value which more than
fulfil the requirements of his commission.

Peter Stothard
Editor, *The Times*

16. It's Getting a Bit Dark

Foreword

The tradition of sending artists onto the field of battle dates from ancient times: great monuments like Trajan's Column or the Bayeux Tapestry were clearly designed by artists who have witnessed battle at first hand. In the twentieth century we have films and photographs to record the actuality of war, but there is still an essential role for the artist. The concentrated First World War images of Nash or Nevinson have the same emotional strength as the poetry of Owen or Sassoon, and future generations will see the wars of this century through the artist's eye as much as the camera's lens.

It was for this reason that the Imperial War Museum revived the official war artists programme, dormant since 1945, in 1973. Since then a series of distinguished artists has recorded the activities of British forces in conflicts both hot and cold. John Keane made a much-acclaimed record of the Gulf War and, as the situation deteriorated in the former Yugoslavia and as British forces, in United Nations guise, became involved, it was decided to send an artist to record that conflict also. However, the Museum's meagre funds were already exhausted and it was an inspired piece of patronage and sponsorship by *The Times* which enabled Peter Howson to be commissioned as the official war artist in Bosnia. The results, seen in the exhibition and in this catalogue, fully justify the choice.

Alan Borg

Director General, Imperial War Museum

Mountain Man
Exhibited at Flowers East

Facing Fear: Peter Howson in Bosnia

ROBERT CRAMPTON

I first met Peter Howson in his Glasgow studio last November. He had made one trip to Bosnia in June and had just decided he wanted to go back. The paintings resulting from that first trip were all grouped at the other end of his studio, while, right by the door, hung an enormous large-scale map of central Bosnia, overlaid with the positions of the British army units there. So the initial impact was made by plastic on paper rather than oil on canvas. Howson pointed out the places that he had seen in June, the places of which we all know and which his art has to make us know better: Travnik, Gornji Vakuf, Prozor, Vitez.

Howson's paint-stained hand moved to the north east, up towards the valleys around Tuzla. He had been following the progress of the war. 'This is where the Muslims are coming back strongly. They're the best Muslim fighters up there . . . I'd like to get up there this time.' And then his hand moved south to Sarajevo, and then west again to Mostar. He wanted to go to both of those ravaged cities, too. Below the map, only half-hidden, like one of the small background shapes in one of Howson's huge figure compositions, was a green army rucksack. 'HOWSON' was stencilled on the flap in white chalk, and he showed me with a little pride that the baggage ticket from Split airport was still fastened around a strap.

Howson had had a rough time on that first trip. The fighting around Vitez, the site of the main British army base in central Bosnia where he had spent most of his time, had been particularly intense, with constant sniping and shelling. The sniping was not confined to the Muslims who surrounded – as they still do – the Croatian-held pocket of which Vitez is the centre: the press corps's interest in Howson, and especially in his earlier than scheduled return, was also heavy, and, despite its inaccuracy, wounding. Howson felt isolated, afraid and, worst of all, unable to work satisfactorily. When I asked him in November how he had managed to work in Bosnia, he said: 'Badly, I sketched badly. That's why I want to go back.'

Howson may be used to scrutinising the faces in the tougher pubs of Glasgow, but the Gallowgate is a mild-mannered place compared with Bosnia. 'Some of the people in Bosnia you knew you weren't safe even to look at, and some you knew were OK. Most of the time, I was afraid to stare.' And sometimes it wasn't even safe to be there at all, let alone look. Howson developed his painting *Travnik* from twenty sketches he made

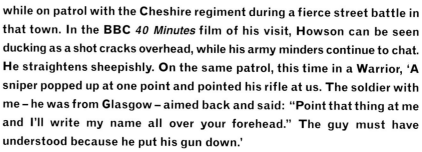

while on patrol with the **Cheshire** regiment during a fierce street battle in that town. In the **BBC** *40 Minutes* film of his visit, Howson can be seen ducking as a shot cracks overhead, while his army minders continue to chat. He straightens sheepishly. On the same patrol, this time in a **Warrior**, 'A sniper popped up at one point and pointed his rifle at us. The soldier with me – he was from **Glasgow** – aimed back and said: "Point that thing at me and I'll write my name all over your forehead." The guy must have understood because he put his gun down.'

Another time, Howson spent the night with a **Croatian** family near the **British** base at **Vitez**: 'I was lying in bed with my flak jacket and helmet on . . . I kept imagining the door being kicked open and these guys wearing balaclavas coming in and cutting my bollocks off or kidnapping me. That happens to a lot of people, masked men coming in the middle of the night and killing them or torturing them. It got so bad, I wasn't sleeping at all.'

Even last autumn Howson's sleep was broken by nightmares. Five months before, his mind blanked by fear much of the time, trying to preserve his sensitivity but clearly finding his imagination a huge handicap in the struggle to cope, Howson had searched for the humanity in the hell he was witnessing. He has been searching for it ever since without, I think, ever finding it. That humanity was most readily available in the children caught up in the war. Children run through his **Bosnian** work, his conversation and his thoughts. Back then in **Glasgow**, he put his hand over the top left corner of a small painting called *Life Goes On.* 'If that wasn't there, this would just be a daft wee scene . . . chocolate box subject.' *That* was a small, smouldering house high up on a hill in the background. 'I just couldn't believe that people were still putting out washing. A woman was killed doing that while we were there.' He was clinging to even the tiniest signs of normality that he saw: 'Everyone told me that **Prozor** was evil, and there *was* an atmosphere of death, but you still got the children waving to you . . .' In his more recent paintings, even the children look like psychopaths.

Life Goes On was a reversal of Howson's usual theme: an innocent dominates a pretty scene darkened by the suggestion of evil. In order to bring that small, smouldering house to the fore, and paint evil on the scale of the epic work for which he is best known, Howson felt he had to return. But there was another, more personal reason, for his desire to go back. 'I can't get Bosnia out of my system,' he told me at that first meeting. 'I talk about it all the time. I'm addicted. It's a horrible addiction. Life is strange if you actually want to go to a place where you could be killed.' He added, articulating an ambivalence that will be familiar to any serving or former member of the armed forces: 'Half of you detests what you see and half of you wants to be there. You're living on the edge and it is exciting. That's the truth of the matter. It's much better than the humdrum existence of

normality.' And much more inspirational. 'Someone said the other day, which annoyed me, that the Bosnian work was important but I shouldn't make it my life's work, which proved to me that unless you go there you don't understand how incredible it is. You don't have a clue. It really could be a life's work . . . there's more material for me as an artist there than the whole of the past fifteen years of being in Glasgow. The sixteen days I was there was the most intense time of my life.'

So, in December, Howson went back. This time, he did not go alone. Two people went with him – his friend and fellow Glaswegian artist Ian MacColl, for company and collaboration, and me. He left his sketchpad behind – 'you can't sketch someone who is utterly terrified' – and instead MacColl took a video camera as an aide-memoire. This time, the heat and dehydration that had undermined his summer visit were long gone, as was, if only temporarily, much of the ordnance. The most dangerous part of this visit was the 150-mile, eight-hour journey up-country through the snow-covered mountains to Vitez. We drove along Route Diamond, the former logging track from Tomislavgrad that has been straightened and widened by the Royal Engineers and now serves as the main supply route – the only supply route – from Split into central Bosnia. You put your kit on, body armour and helmet, just before the half way mark at Prozor, a town that was still as bad as Howson remembered it: 'It's the sort of place,' he said, 'where if we'd broken down we'd have been sitting there just with a steering wheel.' Howson's Land Rover was spat at by old ladies, and the local kids amused themselves by blowpiping a few hypodermics at it. 'Prozor is basically full of lots of ghastly people taking evil lessons,' said Howson. Prozor is the headquarters of the Bosnian Croat army, the HVO, and they know that any convoy passing through is taking food into the Muslim heartland, and they react accordingly, even though the road soon passes back into a Croatian area once more.

The place where Croat territory meets Muslim territory is called Gornji Vakuf. Gornji Vakuf is much worse than Prozor. Being a frontline, it is devastated, the buildings all blown out and burnt out, shells and sniping popping off constantly. You pick up a British Warrior escort at the outskirts of town and it leads you through at top speed. There is a 90 degree right turn in the centre of GV where vehicles have to slow and risk exposure to enfilading snipers on the hillside. Howson pronounced himself 'very impressed with the way the Warrior swivelled its turret and gun round 180 degrees to face back up the street toward the snipers, as if to say "Don't mess with us".' This admiration for the British soldiers on UN duty in Bosnia – it was the turn of the Coldstream Guards last winter – was heartfelt and lasting. Howson, once he had been treated to a No. 1 crop by a Coldstreamer chef, even began to look a bit like a soldier himself, with his Scotch and his Bensons.

Once in Vitez, Howson and MacColl lived on the British base during their
week-long stay. They wore uniform, ate in the cookhouse, enjoyed officer
status in the mess. Indeed, Howson was the army's guest and respon-
sibility throughout. I felt that the closeness of his attachment to the
military might have constrained him. He did not. 'No, I liked being with
them. I felt as though I was back in the army.' Howson, now 36, served for
a short while in the infantry as a young man. 'But this time no-one was
allowed to shout at me.'

Howson spent his days being taken by the British to watch British soldiers
at work – supervising an exchange of refugees, liaising with the United
Nations High Commissioner for Refugees, maintaining the armour that
means that although the local factions might occasionally get cheeky,
they really don't mess with the Brits very often – but his eye and
imagination always fixed on those who have to stay there, rather than on
those who will eventually leave. Having been there with him, I can see
exactly why he did this: your overriding feeling is how puny and irrelevant
and transient is your own fear and presence when compared with the
predicament faced by the Bosnian people. I am sure the British soldiers
feel that too: they have a healthy, self-deprecating modesty about their
role, and a great empathy for the suffering they are doing something to
alleviate. They are not looking for any paintings of heroic Tommies.

We travelled one morning to Zenica, a Muslim stronghold 15 miles along
the valley from Vitez where Larry Hollingworth, head of the UNHCR, has
his base. We were escorted by Captain Harry Bucknall of the Coldstream
Guards. Captain Bucknall, like many others before, during and since our
visit, did a diplomatic and patient job of liaising with the local militia
leaders. Howson could have painted Harry, he could have painted Larry
Hollingworth – a British hero if ever there was one – but he has chosen
instead to paint *The Road to Zenica,* full of the shocked, woeful figures that
we had seen that morning coming out of the mist.

Howson does not find it easy to talk about his work. I have a tape of the
two of us talking while watching some Guardsmen scrub a tank clean of
the mud of an unseasonal thaw. 'Have you seen enough?' I say. 'You've
never seen enough . . . but I think I've finally got it,' he replies. 'What is
it?' I ask. 'I can't tell you.' 'You can't , or you won't?' 'No, I just won't.'
'Can you give me a clue?' 'I'll only know if I've got it when the paintings
start coming.' 'But what is it?' 'It's in the faces, I think I've got their faces,'
he says, and he was not talking about the 19-year-old squaddies five yards
away. Now that some of those paintings have come I know that the 'it' that
Howson saw in the Bosnian face was fear: their fear, his fear – simple and
obvious and yet hard to recognise and capture. This is why, above all, he
went back: to confront his fear, but also to see it reflected in the faces
around him and to control it and channel it into his work. 'If you don't get

the trauma you don't get the art,' he said. 'It's all fear really, the whole thing.'

On the same day, standing there in the slush, Howson and I were joined by a French photographer called Luc Delahaye. Delahaye has won awards for his imaginative and courageous work in Bosnia over the last three years, and so he is a better person than I to make a case for a war artist, in an age when many might think such a job had been superseded by photography or video. Delahaye had seen some of Howson's earlier Bosnian work in *The Times*. 'I would like to do such work, but I cannot,' he said. 'I am beginning to realise that I am limited, that I am in a way misrepresenting the war here. I always have to look for strong moments, and I do not pay attention to the weak moments. They are the most important really, the ordinary things. I am always more bored than excited in this country.' Howson can represent those 'weak moments', that tense boredom common to all wars, in his work and bring out their significance – in a group of refugees just sitting by the roadside for instance – in a way that a photographer cannot, and could not sell to his editor even if he could.

And Howson can do something else. He can do the weak moments, but he can also go beyond even the strong moments, the moments of impact and explosion, to the vile, unseen, monstrous moments of atrocity and outrage. He can put his imagination where no Nikon can dare to go – into the very heart of the Balkan darkness. This is what Howson has chosen to do in the months since his Hercules touched down in Britain once again. He has confronted the evil, and brought it to the foreground. He has painted rape, castration and torture – scenes which he obviously did not witness first hand, but scenes which we all know have been enacted in that conflict, scenes which we have all imagined.

These paintings are bound to provoke controversy. Howson knows that. He says: 'I'm not aiming to be controversial. But I wanted to cut out all the reportage. It's not my job to do that. My job is to do the things you don't see, that the army doesn't even get to see, not to be an illustrator, not to tell stories, but to produce strong images of things.' Even if those strong images do not correspond to anything he saw? 'Yes. It is very difficult because I could paint all sorts of horrible things, based on my own fears, and the fears I saw in people's faces. Sometimes I think I should just do a series of landscapes with not much in them, then I think that's shying away. Another part of me says I should really go for it, do very very frank paintings. I suppose I think I have the right because I was there and because as an artist, I can do anything.' Life is a confusion, war even more so, Howson's version of the truth is just as valid as a reporter's or a photographer's, or a soldier's, maybe more so, because in some sense it is more profound. Truth be told, Howson did not see very much in Bosnia, with his eyes. Nobody does. He did not get to Tuzla, or Sarajevo, or Mostar. He plodded around and found out that war is hell, war is frightening, war is boring, war is hard, and ten times harder if you haven't got a lift home. But the truth is, women *do* get raped in war, men *do* get castrated, children *do* turn into monsters. And Howson *has* seen it after all, in his imagination, and all too vividly. We all have. Wouldn't he be untruthful if he did *not* paint it? Someone has to.

Robert Crampton is Contributing Editor of *The Times Magazine*

9. Smile and Wave

Overleaf:
1. Road to Zenica

18

5. Serb and Muslim

Hound
Exhibited at Flowers East

6. House Warming

7. Deutsch Marks and Derv

3. Sanctuary in Travnik

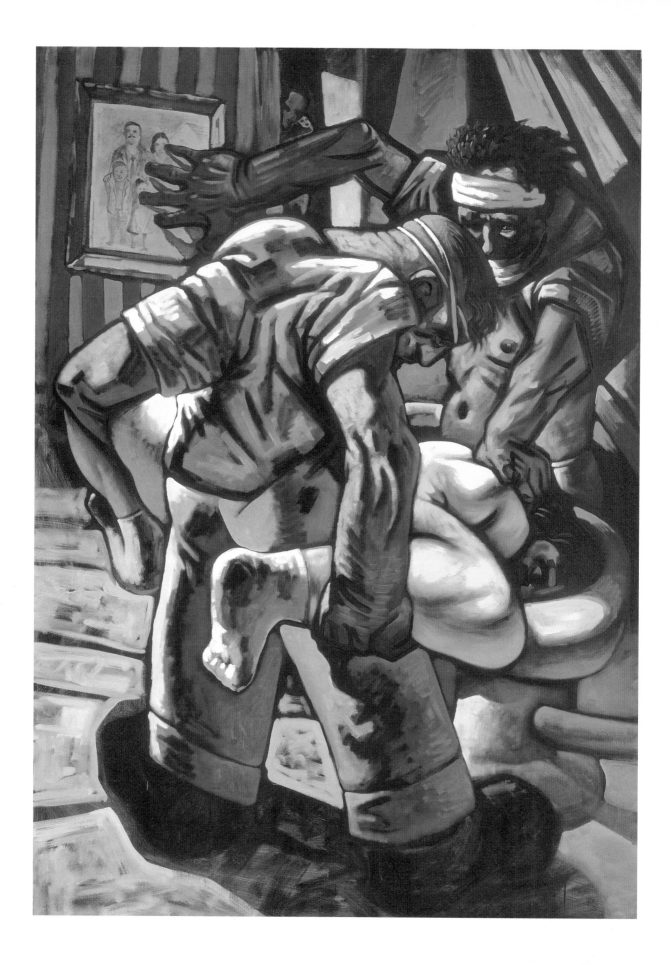

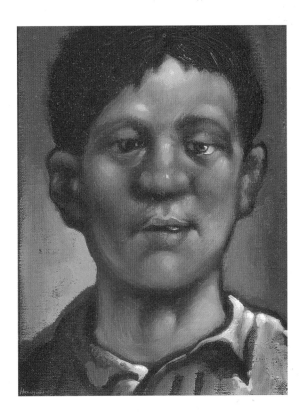

Orphan 1
Exhibited at Flowers East

8. Croatian and Muslim

17. Study for the Cleansing

Monitoring
Exhibited at Flowers East

11. Café Noir

20. Stari Vitez

11

29

Neighbours
Exhibited at Flowers East

26. Roadside

Cleanser 2, 7th Brigade *Exhibited at Flowers East*

32. Bon Bon Alley

22. Life Goes On

19. Gossip

Turbe *Exhibited at Flowers East*

27. Ustazi

29. Christmas Shopping

33. Muslim Fighter on Drugs

4. Plum Grove

Suffering into Art: Howson and Bosnia

RICHARD CORK

Among the profusion of television crews and newspaper photographers covering the war in Bosnia, Peter Howson must have appeared an isolated and even anachronistic figure. While their images were swiftly relayed to enormous audiences throughout the world, he contented himself with modest drawings in the privacy of a sketchbook. Beyond knowing that these studies would form the raw material for paintings executed later, Howson could not tell how they might contribute to the work he eventually produced.

Only now, well over a year after he first went to the war zone, is the fruit of his visits on public display. But the time that has elapsed between initial observation and final creation should not be seen as a disadvantage. The spawning of instant images by electronic media offers no guarantee of lasting significance. Although television commands unparalleled immediacy, and photographers can define a moment with compelling power, there is still a need for the more sustained and meditative insights of the artist. Some now argue that sending a painter to war is a hopelessly obsolete venture. But there will always be a place for imaginative visions unconstrained by urgent news deadlines. The finest war art of the past retains its potency, and may even gain in resonance with the advance of time.

Besides, history teaches that artists often surpass themselves when they take on the challenge of the battlefield. Paul Nash arrived at a sudden and formidable artistic maturity when he confronted the nightmare of Passchendaele. Although he toured the Western Front in the relative comfort of a chauffeur-driven car, his paintings, drawings and prints defined the annihilation of this water-logged, shell-pitted terrain with prodigious anger, compassion and moral authority. Doubtless remembering Nash's achievement, Sir Kenneth Clark hoped for similar revelations when he directed the official commissions of the Second World War. He argued that 'the average artist will probably want to go to the Front, not simply out of curiosity or bravado, but because he may there discover some of the emotional stimulus on a grand scale which is inevitably lacking from his everyday work.'

However much Howson may have hoped for a similar transformation in his own art, the Bosnia work did not come easily. Perhaps the transition

from home to battleground was too sudden and shocking. Life in Scotland before the expedition had become, as he now recalls, 'stale and affluent'. But nothing could have prepared him for the obscenity of internecine conflict. Like Max Beckmann and Ernst Ludwig Kirchner in the First World War, he found this experience hard to withstand. No chauffeur-driven car cushioned him from the distress he witnessed. The spectacle of a country bent on self-destruction triggered an initial revulsion, and Howson found coherent war paintings impossible to produce after his first, profoundly upsetting visit. Time is needed to absorb such a trauma. Many outstanding images of the Great War were only produced years after the Armistice. Otto Dix's definitive paintings were largely completed in the 1930s, so Howson's temporary inability to make visual sense of the Bosnian tragedy is eminently understandable.

In his case, pictorial paralysis did not last long. Following the second trip, he began making a remarkable sequence of small oils. Their modest dimensions may come as a surprise to anyone familiar with Howson's grandest earlier canvases. But he did not feel ready to tackle monumental paintings, and was also wary of reawakening the caricatural strain which had marred some of his largest pre-Bosnia pictures. Perhaps that is why some of these little images avoid bloodshed altogether. In the early 1990s, Howson's most ambitious work had been dominated by aggression. Preoccupied with the spectre of a land peopled by snarling thugs, he concentrated on allegories of despair. In particular, Bruegel's painting *The Parable of the Blind* inspired an extended series of big, desolate pictures. Bent on hurtling to their own destruction, the baleful figures who fill these canvases with venomous energy rule out the possibility of hope. Their very harshness courted melodrama, and provoked accusations from critics of exaggerated pessimism on Howson's part.

Although Bosnia did little to relieve his gloom, it made him determined to convey a whole range of experiences rather than a merely negative view. Hence the variety of moods in his small paintings, where peaceful subjects sometimes occupy most of the composition. In one picture, a seemingly unconcerned young woman hangs her family's washing on the line. Howson handles the scene in a deliberately naive style, reminiscent of a blithe children's book illustration. Only after a while do we realise that the idyllic landscape beyond is sullied, on the far hillside, by smoke pouring out of a ruined house.

Such a painting marks a shift in Howson's vision. He is now prepared, some of the time at least, to counter disaster with a more affirmative order of feeling. Bosnia must have made him aware of humanity's obstinate capacity to survive even the most appalling ordeals. In another, unusually wide painting, a frieze of figures in near-silhouette stand by a road and stare. They might be looking at Howson as he moves past them in his army convoy, and a child raises an arm as if to wave. Their bodies testify to the exhaustion they feel, but the will to remain on their feet appears indomitable.

A few of these preliminary pictures show the moments when nothing happened, and no sign of warfare disrupted the beguiling luxuriance of the Bosnian countryside. Instead, the convoy proceeds through verdant hills without incident, suggesting that the UN presence was somehow capable of bestowing peace on the entire landscape. All the same, the myth is soon dispelled. In one little picture, bearing an unexpected resemblance to a Lowry, girls skip and a drunken man dances in front of houses as innocent as toytown. Then, with a sense of shock, we notice that the house in the middle is a ruin. Once the home of a Muslim family, it is now a shell. But nobody pays attention to the burned-out building, and the air of celebration may be directly connected to the ousting or murder of its former occupants.

In this deceptively festive painting, Howson manages to reveal the macabre reality of a world where neighbourly pleasures and ruthless racial elimination go hand in hand. He does not, however, avoid direct representation of the killing entirely. Stories of butchery were related to him throughout both his visits, and they surface in a number of the most vigorously executed small pictures. One, where the agitated brushmarks look like a homage to Ludwig Meidner's frenzied apocalyptic paintings of 1912-13, is carried out in untypically thick pigment. Ethnic cleansing is here at its most violent, with marauding men gunning down helpless civilians. One of the victims thrusts both arms high in the air, like the white-shirted man at the centre of Goya's *The Third of May 1808*. But the protest is futile, and the smoke filling the sky to an asphyxiating degree reinforces the feeling of universal extinction.

Images of outright massacres are rare, nevertheless. At this stage, Howson seems to have been understandably reluctant to paint scenes he did not witness. In one vivid little picture, the furtive movements of distant street-fighters are contrasted with a shadowy foreground figure immersed in sketching. He turns out to be the artist, sheltering as well as possible from stray bullets but still prepared to risk his life for the sake of first-hand scrutiny.

The consistent determination to observe for himself pays off. It results in images as arresting as snapshots, varying from the laconic to the anguished. On a mundane level, Howson catches the humdrum quality of war by depicting, very simply, a wife and child waving goodbye to a husband carrying his rifle as he walks away from home. But the same artist is equally capable of confronting human tragedy. While Howson and his companions crouched by a brick-stack during a bombardment, a passing woman became crazed by the shelling. There she stands in the

painting, a prime target hiding face in hands as tracers lance through the sky.

Some people, exposed to an outburst of violence, react without any inhibitions. In a little painting handled with a roughness reminiscent of Daumier, two children scream while an older girl tries to lead them away from a burning house beyond. On the whole, though, the prevailing response to the carnage is more stoical. A particularly powerful picture shows five figures standing upright in the middle of a battle zone. One, a woman, covers her face as if to shield herself from the surrounding devastation. But her companions seem far too stunned to take protective measures. They stare towards us, like a tragic chorus daring its audience to empathise with their suffering and share the intolerable burden. In this painting, the well-worn military euphemism 'theatre of war' takes on a new and more painful meaning.

The clearest link between the small paintings and the larger canvases, which Howson only began a few months ago, is to be found in the pair of images devoted to an advancing soldier. At first, they appear identical. Both move menacingly in our direction. Both display a rigid right arm, locked in a tensely aggressive position, and both clutch a can. But then the differences become apparent. While one gazes forward with open eyes, the other looks down. And behind each soldier, Howson has painted sharply contrasting scenes. In one, figures gesticulate against a bleak, smoke-laden background. In the other, girls embrace beside a pool amid a placid landscape.

The two versions reveal an artist struggling to decide how a particularly troubling memory can best be defined. He remembers the soldier now as a 'very threatening figure, coming towards me'. But the context inhabited by this agent of fear has become blurred with time, leaving Howson debating whether to paint a contrasted setting or a location that accentuates the sense of menace. Eventually, in his large painting of the same subject, he plumped for consistency of mood. And the threat is intensified. Staring straight ahead, beneath a white headband which makes him appear still more ominous, the soldier has now developed an alarming swagger. Although he still clutches a can, the rifle slung on his shoulder assumes greater importance. For it is echoed by the child beyond, running forward and waving as he brandishes a similar weapon.

Howson worried a great deal about the warping influence exerted by civil war on the emergent generation in Bosnia. One of his largest paintings takes as its locale a road peopled by gaunt itinerants. Unlike the sunlit thoroughfares depicted in Howson's small paintings of convoys moving through the hills, this one is flat, remorselessly straight and half-veiled by mist. During his travels around Bosnia, the artist found himself staring at

2. Cleansed

such scenes on countless occasions. He made swift sketches of the passing figures, and the people furthest off are little more than silhouettes. The nearest wanderers, however, assume palpable identities. A mournful old woman trudges forward with the resignation of someone striving to endure dispossession and bereavement. She looks defenceless among the men carrying sub-machine-guns nearby, perpetually on the lookout for indiscriminate snipers. But at least she is not saddled with the burden imposed on the young mother across the way, struggling to control her frantic child. Howson reserves the most prominent place in the painting for another boy, who rushes out into the convoy's path. He is the most disquieting figure of all. Looking far older than his years, the child fixes the convoy with a psychopathic gaze. He might well be one of the boys who, according to Howson, ape their martial seniors by throwing syringes at the convoys. The UN presence is unpopular in Bosnia, largely because it refuses to take sides. And its representatives find themselves an automatic butt for anyone's anger. Since he accompanied the military, Howson was identified with his protectors and became a potential target as well.

All the same, he quickly learned how to distinguish his difficulties from the plight of the persecuted civilians. One of the most elaborate and densely worked large paintings portrays a group of Muslim refugees. Driven from their homes at gunpoint by the Croatians, they found shelter with a Muslim doctor before he was shot. So they escaped to a UN camp, where a major refused them entry. He told them to wait for a passing convoy of tanks and use their armoured bulk as a shield during the final run to a safe district. In Howson's painting, they wait for the tanks to arrive, crouching with carrier-bags. Although Howson relied on memory rather than sketches, he gives each apprehensive face the character of a fully realised, individual portrait. Their fatigue is harshly conveyed, and so is their feeling of paralysis. One man pushes out his empty hands, in a futile attempt to plead for assistance. But the UN soldier behind him is bound by the regulations to keep his distance. All the refugees can do is hope that the tanks reach them before a sniper or a bursting shell.

In this instance, the outcome was satisfactory: Howson watched them run to a Muslim area with the tanks' protection. Earlier, he had painted the scene in a small canvas. But he felt no more obliged than his hero Otto Dix to concentrate exclusively on events with affirmative endings. Howson admires German artists' willingness, in the First World War, to depict even the most bestial subjects with unflinching clarity. He could easily have chosen to ignore the stories of atrocities told by soldiers and civilians alike. But to do so would, for Howson, have been a dereliction of duty. There is nothing bland or reticent about his vision of the conflict. He decided, like George Bellows in 1918, that nothing should be excluded

from his war pictures simply because images of atrocities might upset some of his viewers.

Accordingly, Howson did not baulk at the thought of painting the aftermath of a castration. The picture is based on what Croatians told him about the sadistic treatment of their young men after the Muslims kidnapped them. Stripped to his waist and hanging down from the branch of a tree, the abject victim has been left to die. His wound still glistens horribly, and Howson was able to rely on his observation of a soldier's injured arm when painting the gouged flesh. He likewise drew on memories of unconcerned children playing near corpses, for the boy and girl flanking the castrated figure stare at him with expressionless faces. Howson saw for himself how corpses were used as warnings in a constant propaganda battle between the opposed forces. For a few seconds, he glimpsed the body of a dog dangling from a rope. It was enough to furnish him with the image for a painting. Viewed close-to, so that the bullet-holes puncturing its flesh are all too visible, the throttled animal with the protruding tongue is used by its executioners as a crude, public threat. Perhaps they are identifiable as the two figures who, with guns at the ready, stare up at the corpse. Howson could not tell, but the gruesome spectacle certainly made him realise that animals are 'cleansed' in Bosnia as ruthlessly as their human owners.

Many of the victims were impossible to see. Once, when his convoy paused for a rest above a particularly enticing lake, Howson was horrified to be told that the placid water had been used as a dumping-ground for corpses. The beauty of the Bosnian countryside assumed a peculiar cruelty in his eyes, and its presence in many of these pictures is continually ironic. Maybe his awareness that it harboured a multitude of hidden bodies made him still more committed, after his visit, to depicting barbarities which would otherwise have gone visually unrecorded.

The most repellent of these acts centred on women. Howson met more than a hundred female rape victims among the Muslim population alone, and the stories he was told eventually drove him to paint several uncompromising representations of the crimes. The most abhorrent takes place in a lavatory. While one assailant holds the woman's head in the bowl, and steadies himself by placing his hand on a framed family photograph the other rapes her. By including this snapshot, Howson could be accused of making his protest altogether too forceful. But he wanted to show that the violation occurred in the woman's own home, and this device enabled him to do so in a concise way.

All the same, I prefer the paintings based on the artist's direct experience. First-hand observation helps to prevent rhetoric from taking hold, and the most powerful images of women arise from Howson's own involvement

with **Muslim** rape victims whose husbands had been killed. He helped to
lift them onto lorries, and remembers that they were unable to talk about
their ordeals or make eye-contact with him. The moment he chose for his
painting came at the end of the journey, when the traumatised women
climbed off the lorries. It should have been an occasion for relief. But
Howson, in a picture as feverishly handled as late **Corinth** at his most
unbridled, shows how the suffering continues. While a dead child is
carried away on a stretcher, a ghoulish photographer closes on the corpse
without even a hint of respect. An attendant soldier turns away, reacting
with sensitivity to the sight of the child's body. Even so, other figures in
the crowd cannot prevent themselves from staring in consternation at the
women in the lorry. One, with hair prematurely grey, swings her legs over
the side. The movement exposes her shrapnel-scarred thighs, and she
seems bitterly ashamed of her disfigurement.
Some might claim that **Howson** should have avoided such mortifying
scenes. I would argue that war artists have a clear right to deal with the
degradation on its own harsh terms. By doing so, their work may well be
vilified and provoke controversy. But anyone who expects a painter to
sanitise the evils of the battlefield is gravely misguided. Artists returning
from the front line fail if their work avoids the full, rebarbative reality of
the events they have been courageous enough to witness.

Richard Cork is Chief Art Critic of *The Times* and author of *A Bitter Truth: Avant-Garde Art
and the Great War,* published by Yale University Press, 1994.

17. Study for the Cleansing (detail)

Catalogue

1. Road to Zenica 1994
   Oil on canvas
   203 x 319 cm

2. Cleansed 1994
   Oil on canvas
   183 x 244 cm

3. Sanctuary in Travnik 1994
   Oil on canvas
   183 x 244 cm

4. Plum Grove 1994
   Oil on canvas
   213 x 152.5 cm

5. Serb and Muslim 1994
   Oil on canvas
   213 x 152.5 cm

6. House Warming 1994
   Oil on canvas
   213 x 152.5 cm

7. Deutsch Marks and Derv 1994
   Oil on canvas
   213 x 152.5 cm

8. Croatian and Muslim 1994
   Oil on canvas
   213 x 152.5 cm

9. Smile and Wave 1994
   Oil on canvas
   183 x 122 cm

10. Bosnian Harvest 1994
    Oil on canvas
    122.5 x 142.5 cm

11. Café Noir 1994
    Oil on canvas
    122 x 91.5 cm

12. Drunk Man on a Battlefield 1993-94
    Oil on canvas
    25 x 21.5 cm

13. The Fight for Travnik 1993-94
    Oil on canvas
    22.5 x 19 cm

14. Vigilante 1993-94
    Oil on canvas
    46 x 28 cm

15. Three Miles from Home 1993-94
    Oil on canvas
    28 x 46 cm

16. It's Getting a Bit Dark 1993-94
    Oil on canvas
    40.5 x 30.5 cm

17. Study for the Cleansing 1993-94
    Oil on canvas
    30.5 x 40.5 cm

18. Entering Gorni Vakuf 1993-94
    Oil on canvas
    40.5 x 30.5 cm

19. Gossip 1993-94
    Oil on canvas
    30.5 x 23 cm

20. Stari Vitez 1993-94
    Oil on canvas
    30.5 x 23 cm

21. Sheltering from Mortars, Travnik 1993-94
    Oil on canvas
    28 x 35.5 cm

22. Life Goes On 1993-94
    Oil on canvas
    35.5 x 28 cm

23. Study for Travnik 1993-94
    Oil on canvas
    36 x 46 cm

24. Fleeting Glimpse 1993-94
    Oil on canvas
    46 x 122.5 cm

25. Travnik 1993-94
    Oil on canvas
    153 x **92 cm**

26. Roadside 1993-94
    Oil on canvas
    61 x **91.5 cm**

27. Ustazi 1994
    Pastel and chalk
    50 x **65 cm**

28. M.F.U. 1994
    Pastel and chalk
    50 x **65 cm**

29. Christmas Shopping 1994
    Pastel and chalk
    50 x **65 cm**

30. Travnik 1993-94
    Pastel
    29.5 x **42 cm**

31. One for the Record 1993-94
    Pastel
    29.5 x **42 cm**

32. Bon Bon Alley 1993-94
    Pastel
    30 x **23 cm**

33. Muslim Fighter on Drugs 1993-94
    Pastel
    41.5 x **29 cm**

34. Checkpoint Guard with Frightened Boy 1993
    Pastel
    29.5 x **23 cm**

35. Thirteen small Checkpoint drawings
    Mixed media

Further work is on show at Flowers East

Peter Howson

1958	Born London.
1962	Moved to Scotland.
1975-77	Glasgow School of Art.
1977-79	Various jobs, including Scottish Infantry. Travel in Europe.
1979-81	Glasgow School of Art.
1985	Artist in Residence, University of St Andrews. Part-time tutor, Glasgow School of Art.

SCHOLARSHIPS AND PRIZES

1979	Hospitalfield Scholarship.
1986	Prize-winner Scottish Drawing Competition, Paisley Art Galleries.
	Arthur Andersen & Co. Purchase Prize, Mayfest, Glasgow.
	Edwin Morgan Artists' Prize, Glasgow League.
1988	Henry Moore Foundation Prize.
1992	Eastward Publication Prize, RGI, McLellan Galleries, Glasgow.
	Nomination for Lord Provost Prize at RGI, McLellan Galleries, Glasgow.
	European Young Artists Prize, Sofia, Belgrade.

SOLO EXHIBITIONS

1983	Wall Murals, Feltham Community Association, London.
1985	New Paintings and Drawings, Mayfest, Glasgow. Print Studio Gallery.
	Peter Howson – New Paintings, Crawford Centre for the Arts, University of St. Andrews.
1987	Washington Gallery, Glasgow.
	Angela Flowers Gallery, London.
1988	New Works on Paper, The Scottish Gallery, Edinburgh.
	Small Paintings and Works on Paper, Angela Flowers Gallery, London.
	The Twilight Zone, Cleveland Gallery, Middlesborough & Quay Arts Centre, Isle of Wight.
1989	Saracen Heads, Flowers Graphics, London.
	Paintings and Drawings, Flowers East, London.
	New Prints, Flowers Graphics, London.
	Drawings, Tegnerforbundet, The Drawing Art Association of Norway, Oslo.
1990	Drawings and Small Paintings, Agarte, Rome.
	New York, Glasgow Print Studio Mayfest Exhibition, Glasgow.
	Los Angeles International Art Exposition.
1991	New Prints, Flowers Graphics, London.
	New Paintings, Lannon Cole Gallery, Chicago.
	The Blind Leading the Blind, Flowers East, London.
	Recent Paintings and Drawings, The Maclaurin Gallery, Ayrshire.

1992	Gallerie Estiarte, Madrid (Graphics show).
1993	The Common Man, Flowers East at London Fields, London.
	Peter Howson: A Retrospective, McLellan Galleries, Glasgow.
	Peter Howson: The Lowland Heroes and other drawings, Angela Flowers Gallery, London.
1994	Peter Howson: Bosnia, Imperial War Museum, London and Flowers East, London.

SELECTED GROUP EXHIBITIONS

1981	Naked Nude, 369 Gallery, Edinburgh.
1982	Pictures of Ourselves, Scottish Arts Council Travelling Gallery.
1983	Three Scottish Artists, Maclaurin Art Gallery Ayrshire.
	Grease and Water: The Art & Technique of Lithography, Printmakers Workshop, Edinburgh.
1984	Winning Hearts and Minds, Transmission Gallery, Glasgow.
1985	Scottish Drawing Exhibition, Paisley Art Gallery.
	Networking, O'Kane Gallery, Houston, Texas.
	New Image Glasgow, Third Eye Centre, Glasgow; Air Gallery, London (touring exhibition).
	Unique and Original, Glasgow Print Studio (touring exhibition).
	The Smith Biennial, The Smith Art Gallery and Museum, Stirling.
	Five Scottish Artists, Leinster Fine Art, London.
1986	New Art from Scotland, Warwick Arts Trust, London.
	New Work (with Stephen Barclay), Paton Gallery.
	The Barras, Mayfest Exhibition, Compass Gallery, Glasgow.
	The Eye of the Storm: Scottish Artists and the Nuclear Arms Debate, The Smith Art Gallery and Museum, Stirling (touring exhibition).
	Scottish Art Today: Artists at Work 1986, Edinburgh International Festival Exhibition, Edinburgh College of Art.
1987	Scottish Contemporary Paintings, Tuberville Smith, London.
	Critical Realism, Nottingham Castle Museum (touring exhibition).
	The Self Portrait – A Modern View, Artsite, Bath (touring exhibition).
	The Vigorous Imagination, Scottish National Gallery of Modern Art, Edinburgh.
	The Festival Folio, Edinburgh Print Workshop.
	The Scottish Print Open.
	Passage West, Angela Flowers (Ireland) Inc, Co. Cork.
	Small is Beautiful 5: Landscapes, Angela Flowers Gallery, London.

1988   Eighty European Painters, touring Europe 1988-1989.
        Contemporary Portraits, Flowers East, London.
        Figure II: Naked, Aberystwyth Arts Centre (touring exhibition).
        The New British Painting, Contemporary Arts Centre, Cincinnati & USA tour, 1988-1990.
        Small is Beautiful 6: Flowers East, London.
1989   Big Paintings, Flowers East, London.
        Confrontation: Three British Painters, Joy Emery Gallery, Michigan.
        Picturing People, Figurative Painting from Britain 1945-1989, touring Kuala Lumpur, Hong Kong and Singapore.
        4th International Young Artists Competition, Sofia, Bulgaria.
1989/1990 Angela Flowers Gallery 1970-1990, Barbican Concourse Gallery, London.
1990   Flowers at Moos: Amanda Faulkner, Peter Howson, Lucy Jones, John Keane, John Kirby, Jonathan Waller, Gallery Moos, New York.
        21 Years of Contemporary Art, Compass Gallery, Glasgow.
        Mixed Scottish Exhibition, Beaux Arts, Bath.
        Edinburgh Salutes Glasgow, The Scottish Gallery, Edinburgh.
        Glasgow's Great British Art Exhibition, McLellan Galleries, Glasgow.
        21 years of Contemporary Art, Compass Gallery, Old Museum of Transport, Glasgow.
        Three Generations of Scottish Painters, Beaux Arts, Bath.
        John Bellany, Peter Howson, Jock McFadyen, Pamela Auchincloss Gallery, New York.
        UK British Culture Festival, Scottish Contemporary Art Exhibition, Keio Department Store, Tokyo (touring exhibition).
        Small is Beautiful, Part 8: The Figure, Flowers East, London.
1991   Angela Flowers Gallery 1991, Flowers East, London.
        The Boat Show, Smiths Galleries, London.
        Inaugural exhibition, Lannon Cole Gallery, Chicago.
        Human, Surburban Fine Arts Center, Illinois.
1992   Artist's Choice, Flowers East, London.
        Portrait of the Artist's Mother done from Memory, Flowers East, London.
        Small is Beautiful, Part 10: Animals, Flowers East, London.
        Figure in the City (touring exhibition), Talbot Rice Arts Centre, Edinburgh; Mia Joosten Gallery, Amsterdam.
        The New Civic Theatre Gallery, Maastricht, Y'art and P Utrecht, BP Gallery, Brussels.
        Innocence and Experience (touring exhibition), Manchester City Art Gallery, Ferens Art Gallery, Hull.
1993   Castle Museum, Nottingham; McLellan Galleries, Glasgow.
        Glasgow Print Studio Show, Glasgow.
        Scottish Painters, Flowers East and Flowers East at London Fields.
1994   New Work, Flowers East.

PUBLIC COLLECTIONS

Aberdeen Art Gallery
The Arts Council of Great Britain
British Broadcasting Corporation
British Council
British Museum, London
City Art Centre, Edinburgh
City Art Gallery, Southampton
Contemporary Art Society
Dundee Art Gallery
Eigse Festival Collection, Ireland
Fitzwilliam Museum, Cambridge
Glasgow Museums; Art Gallery and Museum, Kelvingrove
Gulbenkian Collection, Lisbon
Hunterian Museum, Glasgow
Imperial War Museum, London
Isle of Man Arts Council
Library of Congress, Washington DC
The Maclaurin Trust, Ayre
Metropolitan Museum of Art, New York
Museum of Modern Art, New York
National Gallery of Norway, Oslo
New York Library
Paisley Art Gallery
Paul Mellon Centre, Yale University, Washington
People's Palace Museum, Glasgow
Robert Fleming Merchant Bank, London
Royal Bank of Scotland
Scottish Amicable
The Scottish Arts Council
Scottish Development Agency
The Scottish National Gallery of Modern Art, Edinburgh
Scottish Television (STV)
Tate Gallery, London
University College of Wales, Aberystwyth
University of Salt Lake City
University of Strathclyde, Glasgow
Victoria and Albert Museum, London
Walker Art Gallery, Liverpool